BEING LIKEABLE CAN BE ATTAINED

Simple Strategies to Build Healthy Relationships and Positively Change the Lives of Everyone You Get in Touch with (Change Your Habits, Change Your Life, Change your mood, Put a Smile)

JOHN P. TYLER

Table of contents

INTRODUCTION

How To Win People Over

There are many people in the world that suffer from the lack of the necessary social skills to attract others in a friendly or erotic manner.
It's not always a simple task to find what the other party involved likes, dislikes or wants to speak and hear about. If this information was known beforehand, we might be able to dress up our speech to get some likeability points.

Nevertheless, there are some simple things that the most important percentage of people in the world are drawn to that can help you attract others to you.

CHAPTER 1

1. Become Genuinely curious about Other People

The very very first thing on the list that is vital for everything to work out is to become genuinely interested in the other person. Great emphasis is given to the real part.
To become curious about others you need to have a healthy curiosity for their affairs that can build your motivation towards meeting them and getting to know them better.
By the term healthy curiosity I mean to possess an interest in things relevant in their lives that you can learn about without crossing any limits they impose.
For example, you'll ask them how their work or student life is going on but proceed with caution when indulging in conversations about their family, love life, and usually things they might want to share with people close to them.
Furthermore, the interest you show has got to be genuine; meaning to be completely real and neither forced nor on purpose to get them on your side. As I've shown before, sincerity may be a top-tier trait to have to seem pleasing.

2. Smile

A characteristic that helps in seeming sincere, kind, and more approachable generally is that of honestly smiling. Firstly, a real smile consists of the widening of the mouth and the appearance of wrinkles around the eyes. only these 2 things happen can the smile be perceived as natural and therefore produce its effects on others.

Secondly, supported Allan & Barbara Pease's book "The Definitive Book of Body Language" smiling sends a submission signal to others.

Meaning that wearing a bright smile makes you easier to approach and have a conversation with because you seem less threatening.
Thirdly, a real smile brings positive energy to the people around you. Don't forget that once we find something amusing we always laugh, meaning that a smile is correlated with having fun. Consequently, people will think that their presence is enjoyable to you and can reciprocate this effect towards you as well.

Lastly, what makes smile such an exquisite trait is that it can even bring its effects "forcefully". this suggests that if you try and smile on purpose, you and therefore the people around you will be more at ease and feel that positive energy filling up your minds.

3. Remembering a Person's Name

I cannot stress enough how this easy thing can work wonders on getting people to like you more. it'd seem relatively unimportant compared to the other things on this list, but its effects are undoubtedly very favorable. As Carnegie pointed out in his book: “A person’s name is the most important word to them”.
Our name is what defines our identity; we've woven this simple word into our minds from the very start of our journey in a way that has a certain connotation for us. It’s the characteristics that distinguish us from others.
By remembering this word, you give the opposite person the impression that you paid attention to them and to who they are. Using their name in your sentences makes your speech more pleasing to their ears.
So, just in case you meet someone or a lot of people at once, attempt to memorize their names by connecting a characteristic of theirs with it or by simply writing the name(s) down to the notes on your phone.

4. Be an honest Listener

This is correlated a lot with our initial point as it is the pivot for seeming truly interested in other people

Listening to other people talking is an incredible magnetic power that draws people to you because of the stimulating effect it has on them.

It's a characteristic that creates you seem like a person that is beneficial to talk to as well as makes other people enjoy the conversations they have with you.

Nonetheless, it's imperative to tell you that this trait also needs to be genuine for its magic to work out. Listening solely for going to the good side of others without being interested in them won't cut it.

Become truly invested within the conversation and other people's affairs, ask open-type inquiries to show them that you want the discussion to go on, and just hear them; with your eyes wide open and your mouth closed. this may make you seem like a very pleasant person.

5. Talk in Terms of Other People's Interests

Directly continuing from above, a facet that gives you an extra push towards people liking you is to speak about matters that interest them.

This could be hard sometimes because you have to find out what things they adore so you can confer about them, also as what they despise so that you can avoid going that way if not necessary.

How is that this a characteristic that can make you interesting on other people's heads though? The answer to that is actually trying to remember the last time you spoke about something you prefer.

When we talk about anything we like we feel empowered since it's interesting to us, and someone granting us an opportunity to translate our interest into words is exciting. Connect this with listening honestly to people and you've surely got yourself a good spot on their minds.

6. Make the opposite Person Feel Important
The last tip on the list is to form people feel important genuinely when in your presence. A surefire thanks to accomplish that is by combining all the aforementioned tips. Engage with others genuinely, find what intrigues them, ask them with sincere interest without taking the lead in the conversation while wearing a wide smile as bright as the sun.
This is one of the feelings you can give to someone so don't be lenient with it; it can make the day for any person that encounters you.

And what it's best is that it's free. you'll make people happy by providing a very small amount of things; isn't that a stimulating trait?

Final Thoughts

Getting people to love you and drawing them to you consists of many simple things to pay attention to and to avoid. But, that doesn't mean it's easy.

As you almost certainly have noticed, for everything to figure out perfectly fine you have to be honest and sincere when implementing anything. Lies and deception can get you up to a specific point, but they're going to unavoidably drag you down at some point.

Sincerely eager to learn about others and wanting to build a relationship with them can make their day as well as give you the social connection you wish for.

"Connection is that the energy that is between people when they feel heard, and valued; once they can give and receive without being judged and when they derive sustenance and strength from their relationship."

EXTRA NOTES

1. Be faithful your word and follow through with your actions
The point of building trust is for others to believe what you say. confine mind, however, that building trust requires not only keeping the guarantees you make but also not making promises you're unable to keep.
Keeping your word shows others what you expect from them, and successively , they'll be more likely to treat you with respect, developing further trust within the process.

2. find out how to communicate effectively with others
Poor communication may be a major reason why relationships break down. Good

communication includes being clear about what you've got or have not committed to and what has been agreed upon.
Building trust isn't without risk. It involves allowing both you et al. taking risks to prove trustworthiness. To navigate this, effective communication is vital . Without it, you'll find the messages you've intended to send aren't the messages that are received.

3. Remind yourself that it takes time to create and earn trust
Building trust may be a daily commitment. Don't make the error of expecting too much too soon. so as to build trust, first take small steps and tackle small commitments and then, as trust grows, you'll be more at ease with making and accepting bigger commitments. Put trust in, and you'll generally get trust in return.

4. Take time to form decisions and think before acting too quickly

Only make commitments that you simply are happy to agree to. Have the courage to mention "no," even when it disappoints someone. If you comply with something and can't follow through, the entire people involved is worse off.
Be clear about what you've got on your plate, and keep track of your commitments. Being organized may be a necessary part of building trust with family, friends, and colleagues. It enables you to form a clear decision as to whether to agree to requests of your time and energy.

5. Value the relationships that you simply have—and don't take them for granted
Trust often results from consistency. We tend to possess the most trust in people who are there for us consistently through good times and bad. Regularly showing someone that you're there for them is an efficient way to build trust.

6. Improve your team skills and partake openly

When you initiate an active role in a team and make positive contributions, people are most likely to respect and trust you. It's also imperative when building your trust during a team to show your willingness to trust others.

Being open and willing to form contributions and to engage demonstrates this. In other words, take what others say into consideration, show that you simply are listening actively, suggest your thoughts and feedback during a respectful way, and demonstrate that you simply are willing to be part of the team.

7. Always be honest

The message you convey should , always be the reality . If you're caught telling a lie, regardless of how small, your trustworthiness are going to be diminished.

8. Help people whenever you'll

Helping another person, whether or not it provides no benefit to you, builds trust. Authentic kindness helps to create trust.

9. Don’t hide your feelings
Openness about your emotions is usually a very effective way to build trust. Furthermore, if people know that you simply care, they're more likely to trust you. Emotional intelligence plays a task in building trust. Acknowledging your feelings, learning the teachings that prevail, and taking productive action means you won’t deny reality—this is the key to building trust.

10. Don’t always self-promote
Acknowledgment and appreciation play a crucial role in building trust and maintaining good relationships. Appreciating the efforts of others really shows your talent for leadership and teamwork and improves the trust others have in you.

On the opposite hand, if people don't demonstrate appreciation for an honest deed, they seem selfish. Selfishness destroys trust.

11. Always do what you think to be right
Doing something for approval means sacrificing your own values, beliefs and principles. This reduces trust in yourself, your values, and your beliefs. Always doing what you think is right, even when others disagree, will lead others to respect your honesty.
Interestingly, when building trust, you want to be willing to upset others on occasion. People tend to not trust those who simply say whatever they think others want to hear.

12. Admit your mistakes
When you attempt to hide your mistakes, people know that you simply are being dishonest. By being open, you show your vulnerable side, and this helps build trust with people .

This is because they may see you to be more like them—everyone literally make mistakes. If you pretend that you simply never make mistakes, you'll make it difficult for others to trust you because you've got created an unnecessary difference between the two of you. When all that an individual sees is the "perfection" you project, they likely won't trust you.

Ways to Build Trust With Your Partner in a Marriage or Relationship

Andrea Bonior, a licensed psychotherapist , professor, and author, shares the subsequent advice for building trust with a partner in a marriage or relationship. Bonior suggests that trust is important for emotional intimacy and that it's necessary for a healthy, close relationship.It's much easier and faster to lose trust than it's to build it up.

As young children, we quickly learn to inform if someone is being untruthful. it's going to be that someone doesn't follow through with their promises, or a parent makes threats they don't follow through on. As we get older , we finetune our expectations and behavior by learning to not trust an untruthful person, which helps protect ourselves from being disappointed again. So, when trying to develop trust during a relationship, don't say things that you simply won't follow through with.
It's also important to not say things that don't accurately reflect how you feel. Consistently telling lies, whether or not they feel small or inconsequential, will end in the other person no longer trusting what you say.
Another aspect of building trust is to become increasingly vulnerable within the relationship as it develops. People feel trust once they rely on one another.

It is also important to be emotionally vulnerable. Getting trust requires you to open yourself to the potential risk of being hurt. this might be revealing things that scare you or exposing aspects of yourself that you don't see attractive . In other words, trust is developed when our partners have the prospect to let us down or hurt us, but they don't.

Respect plays a crucial role in trust. one among the most emotionally enduring ways we can be harmed by our partners is if they belittle us or look at us with condescension or contempt, because a scarcity of respect destroys trust

Any relationship, even between a sales assistant and customer, has a basic level of trust, and thus respect . But maintaining that basic level of respect becomes even more important the more emotionally intimate the connection is

Unfortunately, we often show our partners our bad qualities. We could also be more prone to lash out at people we are close to

than we would at a stranger. We lose sight of the very fact that respect is even more significant to those we love due to the harm that lack of respect over time will cause.
It's not necessary to be perfectly polite all the time together with your partner. However, remember that each time you treat your partner in a way that breaches a basic level of respect, you'll damage the connection you have. Plus, it'll make it more challenging for your partner to trust you over time.
Additionally, to create trust with your partner, be prepared to offer him or her the benefit of the doubt. For this concept , Bonior gives the instance of a patient and his doctor, who he's been seeing for ten years and who he trusts and respects Experts describes the difference between how the patient feels about the trusted doctor's opinion and therefore the opinion of a doctor whom the patient has never seen before. While the patient could also be prepared to have confidence in the new

doctor because of her medical qualifications, it's likely that he will feel a lot more comfortable with the doctor with whom he has developed trust.

It might be easier for him to hear difficult or shocking medical news from his regular doctor because he will be prepared to give the doctor the benefit of the doubt because of the trust and history they share.

One more way to build trust in a relationship is to express your feelings in a functional, helpful way .An important component of emotional intimacy is being able to talk about one's feelings without shouting, verbally attacking, or shutting down the conversation .

Therefore, so as to build trust, develop ways of discussing difficult feelings that are collaborative and respectful. to create trust, you would like to give him or her the chance to connect with the "real" you—which includes your emotional complexity.

Finally, to create trust with your partner in a marriage or relationship, it's important to consider reciprocity . In other words, be willing to offer as well as receive. it's necessary for both partners to feel comfortable with the levels of giving and receiving.

If you've got been lied to or hurt, it can take a really long time to learn to trust again .You might automatically think you should break up with the person who betrayed your trust. However, others might need to keep a relationship going, believing that their partners' actions aren't bad enough to offer up on the relationship.
Either way, it's important to create up trust again after difficult situations, either between you and your partner otherwise you and future partners and friends.
When trust has been broken, like after cheating, and you're trying to rebuild trust, it's going to not be wise to cast all your doubts aside in one go .However, if you continue to hope to rebuild trust, you'll need

to let some of your doubts go, or suspend them, to offer your partner the chance to come through for you.Then, if your partner doesn’t, it's he or she who is disrupting the trust-building.

In any relationship, especially in one that’s been threatened by infidelity, healthy communication plays a crucial role. Each partner should be ready to talk honestly, and if an argument ensues, both people should “fight fair” without drudging up the past

To rebuild trust, confine mind that your relationship may look different after cheating, affairs, or other infidelities. However, it is also possible to build something new, though both partners have to be willing to build a new relationship together.

It is very much challenging to remain in the present and move ahead to the future after someone cheats—it can be better to remain in or worry about the past . While the someone who’s been cheated on has the

proper to feel hurt, angry or sad, if he or she cannot advance from those feelings, it's going to be a sign that the relationship cannot continue.
It is important, although difficult, to trust yourself. Learning to trust yourself and your own feelings and reassuring yourself that you simply will be okay moving forward is the key to any healthy relationship.
Perhaps the foremost important aspect of rebuilding trust after a partner has cheated is to communicate openly.Talk and truly hear each other. Both partners should give some thought to what the other needs. Partners should openly share their needs, and consider whether or not they are willing to meet those needs. If either party feels that they're not willing or able to meet his or her partner's needs, the couple may have to seriously reconsider whether continuing the relationship is the right thing to do.

However, what if you're the one who cheated? for instance , maybe you cheated

on your partner, but you've got both agreed to try and make the relationship work. What does one need to do going forward?
To begin with, take responsibility for your actions. Accept your behavior and assume responsibility for it. Also, have an understanding of how your behavior has affected your partner's feelings. Reflect on your actions, and give some thought to what made you decide to cheat.
Going forward, keep your promises. to point out that you can be trusted, follow through with what you say you're going to do. for instance , if you say you're visiting call, ensure to actually call.
It's also important to offer your partner space during this time. Give him or her the space to precise these feelings to you.
The process of rebuilding trust takes time; it can't happen overnight. Still, confine mind that your partner has no right to treat you abusively. Despite breaking their trust, you continue to have the right to your own privacy.

How to Develop Self-Trust

The fact of the matter is that you can never count on another person 100% of the time. However, there's one person we know that we can count on: ourselves. As Johann Wolfgang von Goethe said,
"As soon as you trust yourself, you'll know how to live" (Fahkry, 2016).
Self-trust is a crucial concept, as possessing it enables you to guard your own needs and safety (Tartakovsky, 2018). It allows you to possess faith that you will make it through challenging situations and allows you to practice kindness toward yourself rather than pursuing perfection.
Self-trust includes having an awareness of your thoughts and feelings and having the ability to express them (Tartakovsky, 2018). to realize self-trust, honor your emotions

and avoid counting on the opinions of others .This allows you to develop trust in your own ability to handle whatever arises. Self-trust is acquired by nurturing our deepest thoughts

Self-trust also includes living consistent with your own standards and ethics and knowing when to put your own needs firsts. Having self-trust requires knowing that you simply can endure mistakes. Self-trust also enables you to pursue what it's that you want.

Avoid people that undermine your self-trust. Often, these people use you, and don't want you to succeed .Although as children we frequently cannot control the negative people we have in our lives, as adults, we will certainly consider whether people support us and whether we actually want them in our lives (Tartakovsky, 2018).

Keep promises to yourself. Honor the commitments you create yourself, whether it's pursuing goals you set or following your

dreams . a crucial part of this is making promises to yourself and keeping them .
One example of such a commitment is creating and sustaining a private boundary. Or, attend bed earlier, or visit the doctor for a check-up (Tartakovsky, 2018). Building self-trust also includes becoming your own ally .
Speak kindly to yourself. Everyone features a harsh inner critic, which sometimes takes the voice of a parent or an educator from your past who made you think you weren't good enough. However, you'll reduce or eliminate the habit of listening to your inner critic. Try being more kind to yourself.
For example, if you create a mistake, you'll immediately think, "I'm so stupid!" Instead, try saying to yourself, "That's okay. it had been just a minor error." Showing yourself compassion once you make a mistake enables you to show a greater understanding of others when they make mistakes (Tartakovsky, 2018).

Self-trust isn't about perfection—you must have faith in your own capacity to overcome a slip-up or failure. Self-trust is nurtured through us connecting with our emotional well-being and listening to any disturbances we may notice .

Ask yourself, "How am I doing?" discover what is going on inside yourself rather than simply dismissing an emotional disturbance .

In other words, be mindful of your inner experiences .Self-trust develops once we honor our whole selves, no matter whether or not we approve of certain aspects of ourselves.

Trust-Building Games and Exercises for group psychotherapy

Jan Brinn from Michigan State University has compiled an inventory of suggestions for building trust and creating a safe environment .Trust-building activities (or icebreakers) are often helpful in situations,

such as group therapy, where bonding or building relationships is required.
The reason of these exercises and games is to help participants to find similarities and differences between the members of the group and to help develop empathy and respect.
Chairs during a Circle
Create a circle of chairs, and ask group members to take a seat down. Invite one person to face in the middle and take the chair away, so there's one fewer chair than there are people in the group. Alternatively, the therapist are often a “model” and whose chair has been removed.
The person within the middle will then share something about himself or herself that other group members may relate to. for instance , “My name is Jayne and that i have been to Japan.”
If other members of the group either accept as true with the statement or have experienced the same thing, they get up .

Everyone standing (including the person within the middle) tries to find a seat on the remaining chairs.
Whoever is left standing is that the new leader, and gets to form a statement. Setting a theme/topic for the statements may be a possible variation for this activity.
Common Ground
Put the therapy participants into small groups, and ask them to speak about what they have in common. Encourage them to consider unusual things, also as the obvious ones. like eye color.
Let the group know that they need 15 minutes to come up with as many common facts as they can. The group with the foremost things in common wins the game.
Tower of Trust
Divide participants into groups and explain that they need 15 minutes to build the tallest tower they can, using materials like 50 to 100 plastic cups, or 10 to 25 pipe-cleaners. After quarter-hour , measure each tower. Which one is tallest?

Then, ask each group to elucidate the process they used to build the tower, the challenges that they faced, and what they learned about working together as a trusting team.

Once a secure and trusting environment has been established, this activity are often used to build empathy.
Get the group with a hat, pieces of paper, and writing materials. Each member of the group will then record his or her personal fears anonymously on a bit of paper and place them into the hat.
Then, members of the group will draw a bit of paper from the hat and take turns reading them aloud and explaining how they imagine having that fear would feel. in any case the fears have been read, discuss how experiencing empathy and having common fears may help teams to create trust.

Building Trust and Credibility in Business as a pacesetter

Building trust isn't just important for one's personal life, it's also necessary within the business world. Small baron Alice Scarlet gave advice in an article on AllBusiness.com about the way to build trust and credibility as a leader.

According to Scarlet, respect is one among the most important traits a leader in business can possess. Leaders cannot earn credibility if they are doing not show others the respect that they deserve. Furthermore, confine mind that a leader is not respected due to his or her power; respect results from an honorable use of that power (Scarlet, n.d.).

To earn credibility, leaders must first show that they're trustworthy. This can't be proved through words. Instead, leaders have to put themselves in positions that show their trusting actions so that followers can believe what they see (Scarlet, n.d.).

To become a reputable leader, you would like to make your loyalty to the people around you evident. If an issue occurs, you'll instantly earn someone's loyalty by taking the blame instead of blaming someone else. You must also be accountable for your actions. Therefore, if you are doing make an error, take ownership of the error . Fix it (if you can). Then, move on. A team won't trust and respect you if you place the blame on them or allow them to bear the burden of your mistakes (Scarlet, n.d.).

Credible leaders keep their goals in mind and always attempt to find the best ways to make those goals a reality. People will only follow someone who features a set goal or destination. Therefore, a part of building trust as a leader is to focus on what the team needs to achieve in the long run and how to take the team to the next level .

Don't depend on words or speeches to win people over. Instead, specialise in your actions to show people what you are capable of. Credible leaders are prepared to figure hard to show others how things are done, or how goals are achieved .

In order to build trust and credibility, show your expertise through your work, and don't depend on the expertise you already have. Credible leaders continue learning throughout their careers to remain abreast of new trends and to stay ahead of others .

Last, but never least, is that the importance of honesty. it's imperative to be honest in order to build trust and credibility as a leader. Basically, if a pacesetter is dishonest, others won't trust them. And, if they lost trust, they'll lose respect too. Eventually, everything will disintegrate if honesty isn't prioritized, so use honesty as a building block of credibility.

10 Trust-Building Activities for Teams and Employees within the Workplace

Trust builds stronger, more productive teams and employees. the subsequent activities were suggested by Justin Reynolds of TINYpulse.com, an internet site used by more than 1000 companies to engage and develop high-performing teams .

1. Perfect Square

Give employees a rope to carry , then ask them to stand in a circle. Blindfold them and ask them to drop the rope. Tell the workers to take a few steps away from where they are standing. Remove the blindfolds, and ask them to travel back to the rope and try to work together to lay the rope out as a perfect square.

2. Back-to-Back Drawing

Pair employees together, then have each pair sit back to back. the thought is that they cannot see one another. One employee is given a blank pad and pencil, and therefore the other is provided with a picture of an obscure shape. Then, it's the task of the employee who has the picture to instruct what to draw to the one with the paper.

3. Night Trail

Put together a mini obstacle course. Then, blindfold the workers and ask them to form a line. Give them a rope and ask them to carry onto it. The team will then attempt to find their way through the obstacle course by relying on one another.

4. Trust Pinball (Suitable to Larger Workplaces)

Form groups of 10, at a minimum. Ask employees to face in a circle. Then, choose one person to be the pinball, and blindfold that person. Whoever is responsible then gently pushes the person across the circle. The one that is blindfolded will eventually bump into employees on the other side of the circle, and these people then gently push the blindfolded person toward the people on the opposite side. The team should alternate with who is blindfolded.

5. Willow within the Wind

Have employees form groups of roughly eight people. One that volunteers to be the “willow” will shut their eyes and let the group know when he or she is ready to fall. The group will then let the “willow” know that they're ready to catch him or her, and with their arms extended, they assist one another to keep the willow upright.

6. Slice and Dice

Have the workers stand in two lines that are facing one another. Then, ask them to carry their arms out so that they intersect. The person at the top of the line then walks down this gauntlet. The team members will their arms one at a time in order that the person can make it through.

7. Scavenger Hunt

Divide the workers into small groups, then ask them to seek out listed items as fast they are able to. Basically, whichever team is that the first to find every listed item is the winner. This activity requires team members to figure together, which fosters trust.

8. The Human Knot

Ask the workers to stand in a circle. Then, have everyone lock right hands with someone on the other side of the circle (to really increase the challenge, ask them to lock hands with the one that is opposite them). Then, have the workers lock their left hands with a different person on the other side of the circle. Finally, the workers will try to untangle the human knot without unlocking their hands.

9. Eye Contact

Employees will alternate staring into another person's eyes for one minute straight. this may help them get better at maintaining eye contact and increase a sense of connection between the employees.

10. Minefield

Separate employees into pairs, and put a blindfold on one person per pair. The blindfolded people, with help from their partner, will then look for objects that are scattered around the room.

CHAPTER 2

Ways to Build Trust With Customers, Patients, and Clients

Building trust with customers, patients, and clients will cause better outcomes in all kinds of scenarios. Here's some advice on the way to build trust with members of each category.

Customers

To build trust with customers, it's advisable to improve security. make sure that customers feel safe when they interact with you.

This now's especially important, given the increase of online businesses (DeMers, 2017). move on social media in order to build visibility and attract more clients. Building visibility through social media also offers a good amount of flexibility—you can engage with followers and clients, post images or videos, or update customers with news and knowledge .

It's wise to under-promise and over-deliver when it comes to all of your customer's expectations. for instance , if it'll take a week to ship a package, you would possibly tell the customer it takes 10 days. Never run the danger of not delivering what you promise . Make customer service your priority. If a customer features a problem and they are given prompt and helpful customer service, their experience are going to be memorable, and they'll be more likely to interact your services in the future. Similarly, consider what would happen if you don't provide that level of service: you'll most likely lose that customer altogether, and it could also negatively affect your reputation .
Set out to make your brand more personal. this might be in your interactions with customers, or in your marketing and advertising. Generally speaking, the more you ask your customers, the higher . Listen and concentrate to them.
Finally, to create trust in your customers, be as available as possible. ensure that your

brand or business is available to customers in some way. Provide multiple lines of contact, like an email and a telephone number , to speak to customers that you're accessible.

Patients

Developing trust with patients helps them feel easier , and allows them to be more candid when discussing their health. Communication is vital . Communicate together with your patients often and well. this may involve getting to know your patients and perhaps learning about their hobbies, families, day-to-day activities, and dealing environments.

It is also very important to be a good listener. Demonstrate this by taking note of all their concerns and asking them follow-up questions.

The second thanks to engender trust in relationships with patients is empathy. you would like to have the ability to convey empathy to patients while still having boundaries that prevent you from being emotionally overwhelmed. Aim to relate to your patients but maintain boundaries in order that their issues or attitudes don't overly affect you.

Finally, instill calmness in patients. Health professionals have to be perceived as calm, competent, and on top of things of the situation (to a reasonable extent). Most patients are going to be reassured by a calm and confident demeanor. Then, if something does fail , they're going to be more able to stay calm as they will trust that you can handle it.

Clients

To develop trust during a relationship with a client, the priority should get on timely and efficient communication. Being open shows that your client is vital to you. At the identical time, you ought to do all you can to help the client feel comfortable being honest with you. you would like them to trust that their concerns or ideas will be taken seriously .

Even if you are stressed or feel overwhelmed, for a client to trust you it's important to maintain a positive attitude. This also conveys energy and confidence which will allow clients to have trust in your work .

Your relationship with a client is professional. However, to develop trust, it's important to acknowledge that you see them as an individual, not even as a paycheck. for instance , show your client that you simply are interested in them by asking how his or her children are doing.

Sharing information with a client is a method to engender trust and confidence. this might include explaining to your client what you did, why you probably did it, and what led you to form certain decisions. Keep your client informed .

The client must trust and rely on you as an expert. Therefore, although it may be uncomfortable, you ought to avoid simply telling the client what you think they want to

hear or holding back your true opinion. Be honest and upfront .
Finally, a method to build trust with clients is to exceed their expectations. Set reasonable expectations, and don’t promise unrealistic results. Also, give some thought to what would be valuable to a client—this can provide clues as to how you can go above and beyond in a way that your client will appreciate.

These four key characteristics distinguish someone as an individual of influence:
1. they're intentional. you'll spot someone who is deliberate by how ready for action they are in their work and life. They prioritize what must be done throughout the day using efficient scheduling and keeping their sights on a long-term view. They also choose their words with care — when it involves influencing, words matter.They steel oneself against their presentations with

research and collaborate with others to offer their best in a given situation. and that they do this consistently by practicing these behaviors on a regular basis with a daily routine.

2. They connect. once you come into the space of someone who is influential, you're included. Sometimes you're asked questions, other times you're offered feedback, all to bring you into the loop – the circle of trust.This connection reminds you that while they're leading the effort, they are doing not choose to do it alone. this is often why you are much more likely to want to collaborate with them and excited about the possibilities of what you might accomplish together.

3. they're resilient. The important person is aware that things don't always go as planned. When the unexpected happens, they're ready to dig in and find new ways to manage a situation. they're also willing to share this new strategy with their team.By taking calculated risks and revealing what

they're facing, you recognize they are there for the long haul. The challenges aren't debilitating, rather they provide the person of influence a chance to reframe, reboot, and are available up with a new plan of action.
4. they're life-long learners. within the presence of a person of influence, you’re keenly aware that they're one step ahead because of how they constantly choose to grow and learn. They never tell you they’ve arrived, because they know there’s something which will interest them around the corner.It is that this passion for growth that draws you to take that next course, stay awake late to master a program, or read a desirable book on your business. you're drawn to their level of enthusiasm as you see the impact of learning for the sake of learning.

The ultimate guide to becoming more influential at work (or anywhere else)

Now it’s your turn. If you’re able to build influence, here are eight steps which will significantly change how you relate to your colleagues, direct reports, superiors, or anyone in your life.

1. Listen without interruption. Listening well is all about your state of mind. once you listen, you're present. concentrate to what someone is saying and not to what you want to say. In fact, practice repeating the last sentence, or a part of the sentence, the opposite person says. This repetition helps establish a connection because the opposite person feels heard — you are listening.Or paraphrase — "I heard you say...." -- to test your understanding and demonstrate that you care enough to understand. Then if there's any confusion you'll know immediately, and you'll request clarification. Being listened to is rare enough that doing so genuinely is probably going to raise your influence with the person you listen to.

2. Act with integrity. When your actions stem from a core value of integrity, you're aligned with your whole self and coherent. From the Latin "integer," an individual with integrity is whole and complete. Acting with

integrity means you bring yourself with you wherever you are: at work, home, within the checkout line. You recognize that what you are doing has an impact on those around you.In addition, you're the same person, recognizable no matter setting. Integrity also implies coherence between your values, your actions, your words — regardless of context.

3. Do what you say you're visiting do. If your goal is to urge others to count on you, honor your commitments. once you say you'll have a response by tomorrow at 9 am, have it in their inbox before that point . Should something prevent you from following through, let someone know that you're thereon and when you'll be able to respond. When others feel that you simply are dependable, you become a reliable presence.

4. Give others a voice. the maximum amount as you'd like to share your ideas, pause and invite someone else to introduce or share a suggestion. ensuring those around you are heard and understood gives

them the freedom to say what they want to say. You empower others by offering them this chance , and that they will feel included in the process.

1. make sure of yourself. so as to be present and lead the way for others to follow, sign up with yourself on a regular basis. This involves physical, emotional, and spiritual wellbeing. Are you exercising and eating well? How about regulating your emotions? Who are the people you switch to when you need to talk? Do you take the time to be mindful and do you pause for reflection? When your needs are being met, you're far more likely to be aware of the needs of those around you.
2. Be relevant together with your skills. Being influential means staying up so far with the latest developments in your industry. you're ready to pivot, if necessary when it's time to form changes. you're also, observably, conscious of the change and

embrace the constant of change.Holding fast to the “way things are done” or “I know best” isn't a recipe for influence in today’s workplace. Observing trends and forecasts, you adapt and reinforce what you recognize and what you need to know. You’re cognizant of practices which will make your business stronger and more competitive.

3. Stay focused on what matters. Removing yourself from minor issues and competition sets you apart as an individual of influence. That’s because you’re far more interested in knowing what makes others tick so they can perform better and more effectively. You direct strategic steps which will take your team to the next level and do your work in a manner that demonstrates exceptional standards.

4. Engage with others. If you would like people to be interested in where you’re headed, you'll do what it takes to relate to them in an authentic and meaningful way. you recognize the names and tendencies of the people you work with on every level and

find ways to bring out the best in them. You tackle obstacles as a gaggle and celebrate wins together. you're transparent enough that those around you feel as if they know you, too.

In the office, it's possible to exhibit traits that facilitate your to be more likable. In my years as a company manager and developing my writing career, I've noticed when people appear more likable and I've tried to develop these traits myself. Here's some to cultivate.
1. Ask questions.I've noticed people that ask questions are often well-liked. It's attribute to be helpful and we all have a great desire to share what we know. When someone appears to wish our help, we tend to love them more because we like being the one who provides the answers.

2. Talk more, not less.A friend of mine may be a small business owner and he is

extremely well liked. one among his strongest traits is that he tends to talk constantly. You never need to guess what he's thinking. He's not blunt or rude, but he explains things intimately . (Being an introvert, i want to develop this trait more in myself–and use texting and e-mail a little less often.)

3. Give your time...gratis. A no-strings-attached approach to helping others also causes you to more likable. consider the person you like the most–usually, it's someone who will facilitate your with the copier machine or is willing to read through your business proposal in a pinch. Of course, those that help just to be liked always reveal a manipulative trait, so ensure you're genuine.

4. Pay attention better .It was mentioned how talkers tend to be more likable, and that's true. Sometimes, over-communicating puts people comfortable . But it's also important to pause once during a while and listen. Good communicators take a breath

once during a while! People that are considered like able are always listeners who are curious to (genuinely) learn new things. the simplest communicators talk and talk–and then listen for a response. that creates them an office favorite.

5. Really and truly care.How does one develop the personality trait of caring? It can be difficult, especially in an age of social media where most are dangerously close to being a narcissist. Caring is an act of setting aside your own interests and ambitions for ages and helping others. It requires effort. you've got to consciously decide you are going to care about someone else. once you do, and you're genuine about it, you'll find that more people will such as you .

6. Admit it, you don't know everything.We all understand how important it is to steer clear of the office know-it-all. Why is that? a part of the reason is we know that person won't ask for our help, and that we like to be helpful. More importantly, those that have

all of the answers are usually pushing their own agenda. In their conceited attitude, they exhibit a way of pride that's not attractive to anyone.
7. choose the laugh, whenever .It's hard to hate a jokester or someone who features a carefree approach to life. Usually, the most-liked people are people who can fill a room with laughter. It may not be in your nature to joke around, and that's okay. Just ensure you are ready to see the humor in something. Be someone who can laugh easily and smile often. You'll win people over.

8. relax .I will admit to battling this one. I'm a significant person with serious concerns! (Most of the time.) But it's better to work out the big picture in life. Really serious people are essentially acting selfish because they focus an excessive amount of on their personal issues. Highly likable people at work are those that can set aside their

concerns and go with the flow. They're selfless.

9. Don't be pushy.Here's a stimulating one–and difficult trait to master. I went on a road trip with someone some years ago, and that i remember how he told me he doesn't have highly distinct tastes. What does that basically mean? For starters, he's not that selfish and won't push his preferences–he'll attend lunch at any restaurant and listen to any form of music. He's flexible. that creates him likable because he will adjust to the situation.

10. Admit your weaknesses.That character on the show Mind Games is right: Admitting weaknesses causes you to more likable. People figure them out on their own anyway. Of course, it's important to not act like a victim or share your problems with everyone you meet. At work, it's okay to travel into a meeting and lead with the challenges you face. People are more likely to suggest some solutions, come to your aid, and even pat you on the rear .

1. discover if they really and truly hate you. Hate may be a strong emotion, one only a few people feel casually. Do they really hate you? Or are you possibly projecting your own negative perception of yourself onto them?[1] [2] That said, the subsequent signs could mean there is some beef between both of you.

* Intentionally making your life difficult (deliberately annoying you, messing together with your work, for instance).
* Ignoring your words and conversations, especially when you're trying to talk with him/her.
* Talking trash about you behind your back.
* Throwing unwarranted cruel language and insults your way at every opportunity.
* Acting rude to you, but being very kind to others. Also, if he/she suddenly acts angry or annoyed around you when he/she didn't seem to be before, that's an indication that they don't like you.

2Dig into the rationale they dislike you so much. Just be straightforward and ask them. 90% of the jerks harboring hateful feelings won't have much to mention back to you -- they're just angry people. When confronted, they'll stammer, hem, and haw, because there's usually no good reason to hate you. But, if they are doing respond, you will have a chance to make things right:
* If they're uncomfortable, just flash them your pearly whites and say, "It's alright . Let's just attempt to be better friends in the future." If that seems a touch condescending, you'll go with, "I understand if you'd rather not speak about it. I just noticed that you simply don't seem to like me and was curious."
* If they tell you a reason why, say "That's good to understand . I'm performing on being a better person, and not doing __________." If you'll give them a concrete step, like you're trying to form less of a mess

in the work kitchen to be more respectful, allow them to know.
* If their reason is unreasonable or dumb, just admit that not everyone's perfect and advance . Don't waste any longer breath trying to tame a jerk who doesn't want to be tamed or hates you for a really immature reason.
* they could say that they "just don't like you". If that is the case, accept that some people just can't bring themselves to love certain others. It's nothing personal.

3Look back on your past few interactions. Did you blow them off? Forget a favor? Insult them casually? Embarrass them? Maybe you have been a bit braggadocious lately without even knowing it -- complaining about a the maid being late when they can hardly afford a broom, for instance . Really dive deep into your personal interactions with them (you're not perfect either!) then try and make it right by bringing up any slights.

4Address the matter head on. Once you recognize what the issues is, you've got to make an effort to fix it. aren't getting snippy and fight them ("I was not rude to you, you were just being a sensitive wuss!"). Smile, be cool, apologize when needed, and make an idea to do better next time. [3] Tell them that you simply know you've had your disagreements, but that you simply just wanted to be straight with them and work things out. most of the people will respect this. If they don't, a minimum of you tried to be mature about the situation.

* Be direct without being pushy. for instance , say one among your coworkers hates you because you backed into his car a few weeks ago. "Listen, I'm really sorry about your car. I made an error , and that i shouldn't have been so careless. I feel horrible, and that i want to find a way to make it up to you."

* If you continue to don't know what caused the problem, say something like, "Hey, I'm unsure what's up, but I've noticed that you're quite upset with me. I hope i have

never done something to piss you off. What's up?"

5Not most are going to like you -- deal with it. For me, this is often a good thing! If you're living your life and staying true to yourself, you are not going to get along with all seven plus billion people on the planet. If you've got tried everything else and the person still hates you, then that's how the opposite person is. there's no way you're changing that, and why would you would like to? Feel good knowing that you put in an effort to change their mind -- it always makes you the much bigger person.[4]

* Ask yourself why you would like to improve your relationship with someone who doesn't like you, especially if the way they treat you affects your self-esteem and confidence.[5]

* Hate is an extreme, passionate emotion. If someone is so invested in disliking you, then they likely produce other things going on in their life that have made them so angry and upset.

6Avoid the person to avoid the hatred. This isn’t always possible, but put them out of your life if you'll . Remove the matter from your life. There’s no benefit to having someone like that around, so block their calls, ignore them on your way within the door, and banish their existence from your brain. Most bullies and haters will run out of fabric once you stop interacting with them. Don't give them some time . Don’t put yourself in danger of verbal abuse.
7Move on. Make friends with people . many other people will like you, and a few people will hate you. That’s just the way the planet works. advance and start fresh with someone new. Don’t let it grind you down, because that is what the haters want. You've already risen above them by trying to form things right. Leave the remainder of the haters in your metaphorical moral dust.[6]
* Remember the quote, "haters gonna hate". Truer words haven't been spoken. Never let

your life revolve around someone who hates you, it's not worth it.

How to make friends

1. Take initiative

Start lecture a person and share something about yourself. Likewise, allow them to share about themselves. There's no have to be so personal at the very first interaction, but exchange some words or stories that can break the ice.

2. Join a replacement club or organization

You'll definitely have something to connect over and some of these relationships might become a long friendships with time.

3. Show that you're friendly

"What qualities are important to you in 'a friend'? ensure that you are exemplifying those."

4. Don't search for similarities

If you don't share an identical vision and hobbies with someone, it doesn't mean you can't develop a friendship. "A true friend is sort of a deep ocean who observes all the flaws of another personTherefore, don't judge someone if he/she belongs to a special mindset. Not doing so will allow you to form new friends."

5. Be an honest listener
If you notice your attention wandering when someone is talking, attempt to bring it back to what they're saying, Guarino explains. If you listen well, people will feel respected, understood, and warmly towards you.

6. Create friendships with friends of friends
This is superb if the goal is to expand your circle,"Many also consider it convenient and safe because they probably share plenty of the characteristics of your shared friend."
7. Stay
Once you've got interacted with a person and exchanged contact numbers, don't

forget to call or message them, O'Brien states. Call them and invite the next meet-up. otherwise you can also communicate over the phone call. Opening up to someone frequently may be a great deal to develop a strong friendship—until it doesn't bother the other person.

8. Say yes
This guideline actors use it too when doing improv and it applies to making new friends, Experts explains that saying yes can appear as if openness to trying new things, but it also can look like just being open to wherever the conversation takes you.

9. Increase your self-confidence
When you are confident in yourself and love yourself it makes it very easy for others to see those qualities in you as well, . Liking yourself and being during a healthy mental and emotional place is an important step before acquiring new relationships. The goal

shouldn't be to only create friendships but to maintain them.

10. Smile
Smiling while keeping eye contact with someone will create a positive effect on the opposite person, O'Brien explains. Talking with a warm smile and consistent eye contact makes the opposite person feel comfortable and interested in the conversation.

11. Find a gaggle that's meeting online
If you do not want to join in-person activities yet due to COVID, Guarino recommends finding a gaggle that's meeting online. for instance , there are online book clubs, business networking clubs, and more.

12. Don't set your expectations too high or expect an excessive amount of from one person
"While creating friendships, I often advise having multiple friends for a spread of

reasons," says Dr. Miller. "One of the main reasons is to avoid co-dependent relationships and those that may develop from trauma bonding. Be realistic together with your expectations."

13. Do a favor for someone
Research has affirmed the positive outcome of doing a favor for somebody , O'Brien explains. It helps in developing intimacy and good vibes between the 2 people. Even alittle act of gentleness can contribute a lot—like providing some sort of help or guidance to the person beside you, whether at work, school or any social place.

14. Ask potential new friends out for "friend dates"
"It may feel awkward or cause you to anxious, but asking a replacement acquaintance if they'd like to get coffee or go for a walk is a great way to get to know them," Guarino explains. "You might click and have an excellent time—or you might

find you don't connect on much. The more friend dates you persist , the more likely you're to find people who are a good fit."

15. Show up
Many times, opportunities for friendships are missed because people fail to be present, says Dr. Miller. for instance , if you're invited out with co-workers, a parenting group, classmates, neighborhood gathering, just go. it's often stated that a large part of success is showing up, this will also hold true in friendships. so as to make friends, you've got to put yourself in the position to create friendships.

16. Try "mirroring."
This can be copying their body language, facial expressions, gestures, etc. This mimicry facilitates individuals liking another person and thus being more interested in becoming your friend.

17. Be consistent

Always Be on time when you make plans with people, don't text them twenty minutes before and say you'll be twenty minutes late, or worse, cancel at the eleventh hour . Little things like being on time build trust in any relationship.

18. remember of cultural differences
As individuals often move for career and family obligations, it's important to understand the culture of friendships within your community. If not properly understood, cultural differences can create a barrier to friendships, notes Dr. Miller.

19. Compliment others
"Spontaneous trait transference" happens when people tend to associate the adjectives you employ to describe other people with your personality, says Dr. Schiff. So, if you describe somebody else with positive adjectives, people will associate you with those qualities.

20. Be curious
Ask open-ended questions. When you're curious about other people, they're going to often return the favor and friendship can be born, Guarino explains.

21. Try a social media or friendship apps
While some people suffer from social anxiety and should struggle with putting themselves in public meetings initially, social media may be a great avenue, says Dr. Miller. There are great groups that align with various interests. Also, there are some free apps that, a bit like dating, connect friends

22. If you're during a good mood, show it.
People are strongly influenced by the moods of people and can even unconsciously feel the emotions of those around them, Dr. Schiff states. Do your best to speak positive emotions so others feel happy when they're around you.

www.ingramcontent.com/pod-product-compliance
Lightning Source LLC
LaVergne TN
LVHW050340160826
845677LV00014B/3699